A Child's Garden of Verses

A Child's Garden of Verses

ROBERT LOUIS STEVENSON

Illustrated by Michael Foreman

DELACORTE PRESS/NEW YORK

——————— FOR BEN ———————

Published by
Delacorte Press
1 Dag Hammarskjold Plaza
New York, New York 10017

Illustrations copyright © 1985 by Michael Foreman

Introduction copyright © 1985 by Mary Thwaite

Manufactured in Italy

First U.S.A. printing

ISBN: 0-385-29430-1

CONTENTS

Introduction	*page*	12
Dedication		15
Bed in Summer		17
A Thought		17
At the Seaside		18
Young Night Thought		19
Whole Duty of Children		20
Rain		20
Pirate Story		21
Foreign Lands		22
Windy Nights		24
Travel		25
Singing		28
Looking Forward		28
A Good Play		29
Where Go the Boats?		30
Auntie's Skirts		30
The Land of Counterpane		31
The Land of Nod		33
My Shadow		34
System		36
A Good Boy		37
Escape at Bedtime		38
Marching Song		40
The Cow		41
Happy Thought		42

The Wind   43

Keepsake Mill   44

Good and Bad Children   46

Foreign Children   48

The Sun's Travels   49

The Lamplighter   50

My Bed is a Boat   52

The Moon   53

The Swing   54

Time to Rise   55

Looking-glass River   56

Fairy Bread   58

From a Railway Carriage   60

Winter-time   61

The Hayloft   64

Farewell to the Farm   65

North-West Passage:

   1. Good Night   66

   2. Shadow March   68

   3. In Port   69

THE CHILD ALONE

The Unseen Playmate   73

My Ship and I   74

My Kingdom   76

Picture-books in Winter   78

My Treasures 80

Block City 81

The Land of Story-books 83

Armies in the Fire 85

The Little Land 86

GARDEN DAYS

Night and Day 93

Nest Eggs 96

The Flowers 98

Summer Sun 99

The Dumb Soldier 100

Autumn Fires 102

The Gardener 103

Historical Associations 104

ENVOYS

To Willie and Henrietta 109

To My Mother 110

To Auntie 111

To Minnie 112

To My Name-Child 116

To Any Reader 118

This classic for children has pleased readers of every generation since it was first published in 1885. The writer, Robert Louis Stevenson, was a craftsman of letters, well-known in the literary circles of his day, but now chiefly remembered for this book of verses about his childhood, and for the adventure stories he wrote for young people – especially *Treasure Island*.

Born in Edinburgh in 1850, Robert Louis Stevenson was an only child. His father, Thomas Stevenson, followed the family profession of engineer and designer of lighthouses, and he expected his son to maintain the tradition, but it was not to be. His mother was the youngest of the thirteen children of the Rev. Lewis Balfour, minister at Colinton, near Edinburgh. Young Louis spent happy summers there at his grandfather's home, with some of his many cousins – the "Minnie", "Henrietta", "Willie" of the Envoys, and others. Here the children created a life of play and imaginary adventures beside the river (the Water of Leith), by the churchyard, and in the golden sunlight of the sloping lawn – the "Arcadia" that illumines some of these "rhymes of old delight", in which the fun and wild imaginings are linked with the small, safe realities of the Edinburgh home, and "happy, chimney corner-days".

Stevenson's childhood was active and happy, in spite of much illness caused by a lung weakness which was to affect him all his life, but little of childish illness is reflected in these cheerful verses. Only in the dedication to his nurse, "To Alison Cunningham, from her Boy", do we discover how familiar was "the land of counterpane" in Louis' early years. It was "Cummie" who cared tenderly for the sick child during his long nights of coughing and wakefulness, "made bearable by her unwearied sympathy". She influenced the boy, too, by her "Covenanting" faith, and her lively, dramatic way of reading to him religious stories and verses. So that when *A Child's Garden of Verses* was being prepared for publication he told her that she was the only person who would understand it. She had made his childhood happy, "so it was right that it should be dedicated to no other person . . ."

Much of Stevenson's adult life was spent in wandering, in search of a climate healthier than that of cool, damp Scotland, although it was in the rainy Highland summer of 1881 while he was staying at Braemar, that he began to write the poems. He had returned there from America, after his marriage to Fanny Osbourne the previous year. From his mother's account it seems that he was inspired by Kate Greenaway's *Birthday Book for Children*, published in 1880, with verses by Mrs. Sale Barker. Louis had looked at this and decided he would try his hand. But after seventeen numbers, these "Penny Whistles", as he later named them, were left unfinished, because in September 1881 he had also begun a tale of adventure to please his schoolboy stepson, Lloyd Osbourne – the famous *Treasure Island*, hurriedly being prepared for serialisation that October.

Two years went by before Stevenson turned to the verses again. By then he and his wife had found a home for a while on the French Riviera, and there, while recovering from a serious lung haemorrhage, he began to make additions to the rhymes and jingles, much handicapped by having to write with his left hand. They soon numbered forty-eight, and were actually set up in type, but not then printed. Here at Chalet La Solitude, above Hyères, Stevenson found domestic happiness, and happiness, too, in recreating those well-remembered childhood days, still aglow with an unfaded brightness.

In 1884 ill-health began to threaten Louis more seriously, and he also became concerned about his aging father, so he and Fanny returned to England. It was at Bournemouth that *A Child's Garden of Verses* reached its final form, and the small volume of sixty-seven poems, plainly printed without illustrations, was published by Longmans Green in March 1885. It had an immediate and enduring success.

It was hoped that one of the famous picture book illustrators of the day might have been available to adorn the words, but nothing came of this. It was ten years later, at the end of 1895 (and a year after Stevenson's death in Samoa, where the writer had finally made his home), that the first illustrated version was issued by John Lane, with decorative, end-of-century style drawings by Charles Robinson.

"I am one of the few people in the world who do not forget their own lives", Stevenson wrote in a letter to a friend. His clear recall of childish memories and the ability to bring them to life with "the bright ring of words" created in *A Child's Garden of Verses* something far greater than another book about the life of childhood. This new Centenary edition, with its exquisite and evocative pictures by Michael Foreman, presents the verses in all their freshness and charm for a new generation. Readers now may know little of the gas lamps, the swaying hills of hay, or the panting, smoking trains of little Louis' world. But the "child of air" still haunts the garden, and his songs endure, for they belong to that magical country that lies outside our prison of modernity.

Mary Thwaite, *May 1985*

TO ALISON CUNNINGHAM
FROM HER BOY

For the long nights you lay awake
And watched for my unworthy sake:
For your most comfortable hand
That led me through the uneven land:
For all the story-books you read,
For all the pains you comforted,
For all you pitied, all you bore,
In sad and happy days of yore: –
My second Mother, my first Wife,
The angel of my infant life –
From the sick child, now well and old,
Take, nurse, the little book you hold!

And grant it, Heaven, that all who read
May find as dear a nurse at need,
And every child who lists my rhyme,
In the bright fireside, nursery clime,
May hear it in as kind a voice
As made my childish days rejoice!

R.L.S.

BED IN SUMMER

In winter I get up at night
And dress by yellow candle-light.
In summer, quite the other way,
I have to go to bed by day.

I have to go to bed and see
The birds still hopping on the tree,
Or hear the grown-up people's feet
Still going past me in the street.

And does it not seem hard to you,
When all the sky is clear and blue,
And I should like so much to play,
To have to go to bed by day?

A THOUGHT

It is very nice to think
The world is full of meat and drink,
With little children saying grace
In every Christian kind of place.

—— AT THE SEASIDE ——

When I was down beside the sea
A wooden spade they gave to me
   To dig the sandy shore.
My holes were empty like a cup,
In every hole the sea came up
   Till it could come no more.

YOUNG NIGHT THOUGHT

All night long, and every night,
When my mamma puts out the light,
I see the people marching by,
As plain as day, before my eye.

Armies and emperors and kings,
All carrying different kinds of things,
And marching in so grand a way,
You never saw the like by day.

So fine a show was never seen
At the great circus on the green;
For every kind of beast and man
Is marching in that caravan.

At first they move a little slow,
But still the faster on they go,
And still beside them close I keep
Until we reach the town of Sleep.

WHOLE DUTY OF CHILDREN

A child should always say what's true,
And speak when he is spoken to,
And behave mannerly at table:
At least as far as he is able.

—— RAIN ——

The rain is raining all around,
    It falls on field and tree,

It rains on the umbrellas here,
    And on the ships at sea.

Three of us afloat in the meadow by the swing,
  Three of us aboard in the basket on the lea.
Winds are in the air, they are blowing in the spring,
  And waves are on the meadows like the waves there
    are at sea.

Where shall we adventure, to-day that we're afloat,
  Wary of the weather and steering by a star?
Shall it be to Africa, a-steering of the boat,
  To Providence, or Babylon, or off to Malabar?

Hi! but here's a squadron a-rowing on the sea –
  Cattle on the meadow a-charging with a roar!
Quick, and we'll escape them, they're as mad as they
    can be.
  The wicket is the harbour and the garden is the shore.

FOREIGN LANDS

Up into the cherry-tree
Who should climb but little me?
I held the trunk with both my hands
And looked abroad on foreign lands.

I saw the next-door garden lie,
Adorned with flowers before my eye,
And many pleasant places more
That I had never seen before.

I saw the dimpling river pass
And be the sky's blue looking-glass;
The dusty roads go up and down
With people tramping in to town.

If I could find a higher tree
Farther and farther I should see,
To where the grown-up river slips
Into the sea among the ships,

To where the roads on either hand
Lead onward into fairy land,
Where all the children dine at five,
And all the playthings come alive.

WINDY NIGHTS

Whenever the moon and stars are set,
    Whenever the wind is high,
All night long in the dark and wet,
    A man goes riding by.
Late in the night when the fires are out,
Why does he gallop and gallop about?

Whenever the trees are crying aloud,
    And ships are tossed at sea,
By, on the highway, low and loud,
    By at the gallop goes he.
By at the gallop he goes, and then
By he comes back at the gallop again.

I should like to rise and go
Where the golden apples grow;
Where below another sky
Parrot islands anchored lie,
And, watched by cockatoos and goats,
Lonely Crusoes building boats;
Where in sunshine reaching out
Eastern cities, miles about,
Are with mosque and minaret
Among sandy gardens set,
And the rich goods from near and far
Hang for sale in the bazaar;
Where the Great Wall round China goes,
And on one side the desert blows,
And with bell and voice and drum,
Cities on the other hum;

Where are forests, hot as fire,
Wide as England, tall as a spire,
Full of apes and coco-nuts
And the negro hunters' huts;
Where the knotty crocodile
Lies and blinks in the Nile,
And the red flamingo flies

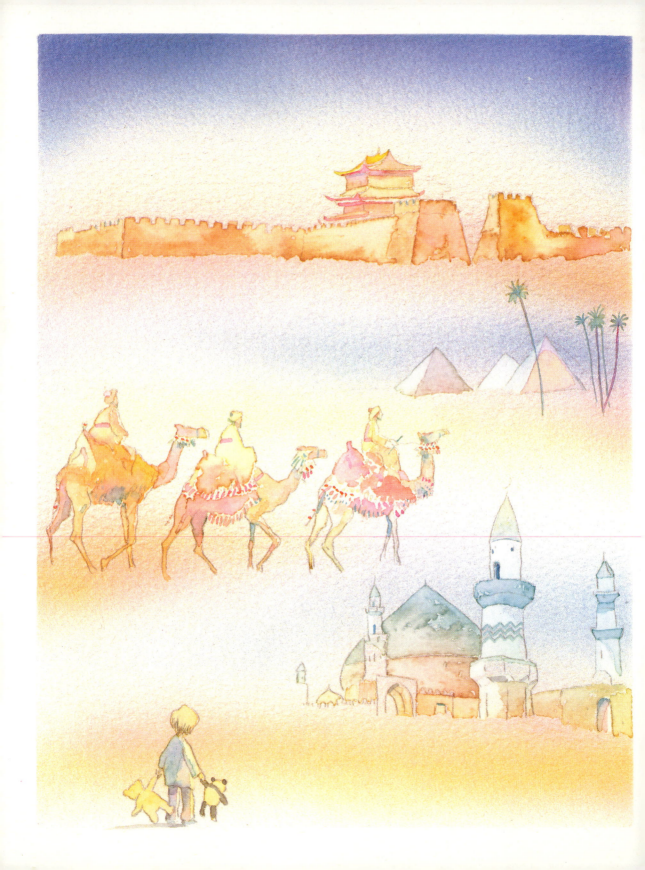

Hunting fish before his eyes;
Where in jungles, near and far,
Man-devouring tigers are,
Lying close and giving ear
Lest the hunt be drawing near,
Or a comer-by be seen
Swinging in a palanquin;
Where among the desert sands
Some deserted city stands,

All its children, sweep and prince,
Grown to manhood ages since,
Not a foot in street or house,
Not a stir of child or mouse,
And when kindly falls the night,
In all the town no spark of light.
There I'll come when I'm a man
With a camel caravan;
Light a fire in the gloom
Of some dusty dining-room;
See the pictures on the walls,
Heroes, fights and festivals;
And in a corner find the toys
Of the old Egyptian boys.

Of speckled eggs the birdie sings
  And nests among the trees;
The sailor sings of ropes and things
  In ships upon the seas.

The children sing in far Japan,
  The children sing in Spain;
The organ with the organ man
  Is singing in the rain.

LOOKING FORWARD

When I am grown to man's estate
I shall be very proud and great,
And tell the other girls and boys
Not to meddle with my toys.

A GOOD PLAY

We built a ship upon the stairs
All made of the back-bedroom chairs,
And filled it full of sofa pillows
To go a-sailing on the billows.

We took a saw and several nails,
And water in the nursery pails;
And Tom said, 'Let us also take
An apple and a slice of cake';
Which was enough for Tom and me
To go a-sailing on, till tea.

We sailed along for days and days,
And had the very best of plays;
But Tom fell out and hurt his knee,
So there was no one left but me.

WHERE GO THE BOATS?

Dark brown is the river,
    Golden is the sand.
It flows along for ever,
    With trees on either hand.

Green leaves a-floating,
    Castles of the foam,
Boats of mine a-boating –
    Where will all come home?

On goes the river
    And out past the mill,
Away down the valley,
    Away down the hill.

Away down the river,
    A hundred miles or more,
Other little children
    Shall bring my boats ashore.

—— AUNTIE'S SKIRTS ——

Whenever Auntie moves around,
Her dresses make a curious sound;
They trail behind her up the floor,
And trundle after through the door.

THE LAND OF COUNTERPANE

When I was sick and lay a-bed,
I had two pillows at my head,
And all my toys beside me lay
To keep me happy all the day.

And sometimes for an hour or so
I watched my leaden soldiers go,

With different uniforms and drills,
Among the bed-clothes, through the hills;

And sometimes sent my ships in fleets
All up and down among the sheets;
Or brought my trees and houses out,
And planted cities all about.

I was the giant great and still
That sits upon the pillow-hill,
And sees before him, dale and plain,
The pleasant land of counterpane.

THE LAND OF NOD

From breakfast on all through the day
At home among my friends I stay;
But every night I go abroad
Afar into the land of Nod.

All by myself I have to go,
With none to tell me what to do –
All alone beside the streams
And up the mountain-sides of dreams.

The strangest things are there for me,
Both things to eat and things to see,
And many frightening sights abroad
Till morning in the land of Nod.

Try as I like to find the way,
I never can get back by day,
Nor can remember plain and clear
The curious music that I hear.

MY SHADOW

I have a little shadow that goes in and out with me,
And what can be the use of him is more than I can see.
He is very, very like me from the heels up to the head;
And I see him jump before me, when I jump into my bed.

The funniest thing about him is the way he likes to grow –
Not at all like proper children, which is always very slow;
For he sometimes shoots up taller like an india-rubber
    ball,
And he sometimes gets so little that there's none of him
    at all.

He hasn't got a notion of how children ought to play,
And can only make a fool of me in every sort of way.
He stays so close beside me, he's a coward you can see;
I'd think shame to stick to nursie as that shadow sticks
    to me!

One morning, very early, before the sun was up,
I rose and found the shining dew on every buttercup;
But my lazy little shadow, like an arrant sleepy-head,
Had stayed at home behind me and was fast asleep in bed.

SYSTEM

Every night my prayers I say,
And get my dinner every day;
And every day that I've been good,
I get an orange after food.

The child that is not clean and neat,
With lots of toys and things to eat,
He is a naughty child, I'm sure —
Or else his dear papa is poor.

I woke before the morning, I was happy all the day,
I never said an ugly word, but smiled and stuck to play.

And now at last the sun is going down behind the wood,
And I am very happy, for I know that I've been good.

My bed is waiting cool and fresh, with linen smooth
    and fair,
And I must off to sleepsin-by, and not forget my prayer.

I know that, till to-morrow I shall see the sun arise,
No ugly dream shall fright my mind, no ugly sight
    my eyes,

But slumber hold me tightly till I waken in the dawn,
And hear the thrushes singing in the lilacs round
    the lawn.

The lights from the parlour and kitchen shone out
    Through the blinds and the windows and bars;
And high overhead and all moving about,
    There were thousands of millions of stars.
There ne'er were such thousands of leaves on a tree,
    Nor of people in church or the Park,
As the crowds of the stars looked down upon me,
    And that glittered and winked in the dark.

The Dog, and the Plough, and the Hunter, and all,
    And the star of the sailor, and Mars,
These shone in the sky, and the pail by the wall
    Would be half full of water and stars.
They saw me at last, and they chased me with cries,
    And they soon had me packed into bed;
But the glory kept shining and bright in my eyes,
    And the stars going round in my head.

— MARCHING SONG —

Bring the comb and play upon it!
　　Marching, here we come!
Willie cocks his highland bonnet,
　　Johnnie beats the drum.

Mary Jane commands the party,
　　Peter leads the rear;
Feet in time, alert and hearty,
　　Each a Grenadier!

All in the most martial manner
　　Marching double-quick;
While the napkin like a banner
　　Waves upon the stick!

THE COW

The friendly cow, all red and white,
    I love with all my heart:
She gives me cream with all her might,
    To eat with apple-tart.

She wanders lowing here and there,
    And yet she cannot stray,
All in the pleasant open air,
    The pleasant light of day;

And blown by all the winds that pass
    And wet with all the showers,
She walks among the meadow grass
    And eats the meadow flowers.

HAPPY THOUGHT

The world is so full
    of a number of things,
I'm sure we should all
    be as happy as kings.

THE WIND

I saw you toss the kites on high
And blow the birds about the sky;
And all around I heard you pass,
Like ladies' skirts across the grass –
    O wind, a-blowing all day long,
    O wind, that sings so loud a song!

I saw the different things you did,
But always you yourself you hid.
I felt you push, I heard you call,
I could not see yourself at all –
    O wind, a-blowing all day long,
    O wind, that sings so loud a song!

O you that are so strong and cold,
O blower, are you young or old?
Are you a beast of field and tree,
Or just a stronger child than me?
    O wind, a-blowing all day long,
    O wind, that sings so loud a song!

KEEPSAKE MILL

Over the borders, a sin without pardon,
   Breaking the branches and crawling below,
Out through the breach in the wall of the garden,
   Down by the banks of the river, we go.

Here is the mill with the humming of thunder,
   Here is the weir with the wonder of foam,
Here is the sluice with the race running under –
   Marvellous places, though handy to home!

Sounds of the village grow stiller and stiller,
    Stiller the note of the birds on the hill;
Dusty and dim are the eyes of the miller,
    Deaf are his ears with the moil of the mill.

Years may go by, and the wheel in the river
    Wheel as it wheels for us, children, to-day,
Wheel and keep roaring and foaming for ever
    Long after all of the boys are away.

Home from the Indies, and home from the ocean,
    Heroes and soldiers we all shall come home;
Still we shall find the old mill-wheel in motion,
    Turning and churning that river to foam.

You with the bean that I gave when we quarrelled,
    I with your marble of Saturday last,
Honoured and old and all gaily apparelled,
    Here we shall meet and remember the past.

GOOD AND BAD CHILDREN

Children, you are very little,
And your bones are very brittle;
If you would grow great and stately,
You must try to walk sedately.

You must still be bright and quiet,
And content with simple diet;
And remain, through all bewild'ring,
Innocent and honest children.

Happy hearts and happy faces,
Happy play in grassy places –

That was how, in ancient ages,
Children grew to kings and sages.

But the unkind and the unruly,
And the sort to eat unduly,
They must never hope for glory –
Theirs is quite a different story!

Cruel children, crying babies,
All grow up as geese and gabies,
Hated, as their age increases,
By their nephews and their nieces

— FOREIGN CHILDREN —

Little Indian, Sioux or Crow,
Little frosty Eskimo,
Little Turk or Japanee,
O! don't you wish that you were me?

You have seen the scarlet trees
And the lions over seas;
You have eaten ostrich eggs,
And turned the turtles off their legs.

Such a life is very fine,
But it's not so nice as mine;
You must often, as you trod,
Have wearied *not* to be abroad.

You have curious things to eat,
I am fed on proper meat;
You must dwell beyond the foam,
But I am safe and live at home.

Little Indian, Sioux or Crow,
Little Frosty Eskimo,
Little Turk or Japanee,
O! don't you wish that you were me?

The sun is not a-bed when I
At night upon my pillow lie;
Still round the earth his way he takes,
And morning after morning makes.

While here at home, in shining day,
We round the sunny garden play,
Each little Indian sleepy-head
Is being kissed and put to bed.

And when at eve I rise from tea,
Day dawns beyond the Atlantic Sea,
And all the children in the West
Are getting up and being dressed.

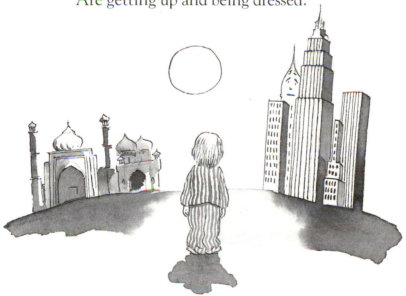

— THE LAMPLIGHTER —

My tea is nearly ready
   and the sun has left the sky;
It's time to take the window
   to see Leerie going by;
For every night at tea-time
   and before you take your seat,
With lantern and with ladder
   he comes posting up the street.

Now Tom would be a driver
   and Maria go to sea,
And my papa's a banker
   and as rich as he can be;
But I, when I am stronger
   and can choose what I'm to do,
O Leerie, I'll go round at night
   and light the lamps with you!

For we are very lucky,
   with a lamp before the door,
And Leerie stops to light it
   as he lights so many more;
And O! before you hurry by
   with ladder and with light,
O Leerie, see a little child
   and nod to him to-night!

MY BED IS A BOAT

My bed is like a little boat;
  Nurse helps me in when I embark;
She girds me in my sailor's coat
  And starts me in the dark.

At night, I go on board and say
  Good-night to all my friends on shore;
I shut my eyes and sail away
  And see and hear no more.

And sometimes things to bed I take,
  As prudent sailors have to do;
Perhaps a slice of wedding-cake,
  Perhaps a toy or two.

All night across the dark we steer:
  But when the day returns at last,
Safe in my room, beside the pier,
  I find my vessel fast.

THE MOON

The moon has a face like the clock in the hall;
She shines on thieves on the garden wall,
On streets and fields and harbour quays,
And birdies asleep in the forks of the trees.

The squalling cat and the squeaking mouse,
The howling dog by the door of the house,
The bat that lies in bed at noon,
All love to be out by the light of the moon.

But all of the things that belong to the day
Cuddle to sleep to be out of her way;
And flowers and children close their eyes
Till up in the morning the sun shall rise.

THE SWING

How do you like to go up in a swing,
   Up in the air so blue?
Oh, I do think it the pleasantest thing
   Ever a child can do!

Up in the air and over the wall,
   Till I can see so wide,
Rivers and trees and cattle and all
   Over the countryside –

Till I look down on the garden green,
   Down on the roof so brown –
Up in the air I go flying again,
   Up in the air and down!

A birdie with a yellow bill
Hopped upon the window sill.
Cocked his shining eye and said:
'Ain't you 'shamed, you sleepy-head?'

LOOKING-GLASS RIVER

Smooth it slides upon its travel,
   Here a wimple, there a gleam –
     O the clean gravel!
     O the smooth stream!

Sailing blossoms, silver fishes,
   Paven pools as clear as air –
     How a child wishes
     To live down there!

We can see our coloured faces
   Floating on the shaken pool
     Down in cool places,
     Dim and very cool;

Till a wind or water wrinkle,
    Dipping marten, plumping trout,
        Spreads in a twinkle
        And blots all out.

See the rings pursue each other;
    All below grows black as night,
        Just as if mother
        Had blown out the light!

Patience, children, just a minute –
    See the spreading circles die;
        The stream and all in it
        Will clear by-and-by.

—— FAIRY BREAD ——

Come up here, O dusty feet!
    Here is fairy bread to eat.
Here in my retiring room,
    Children, you may dine
On the golden smell of broom
    And the shade of pine;
And when you have eaten well,
Fairy stories hear and tell.

— FROM A RAILWAY CARRIAGE —

Faster than fairies, faster than witches,
Bridges and houses, hedges and ditches;
And charging along like troops in a battle,
All through the meadows the horses and cattle:
All of the sights of the hill and the plain
Fly as thick as driving rain;
And ever again, in the wink of an eye,
Painted stations whistle by.

Here is a child who clambers and scrambles,
All by himself and gathering brambles;
Here is a tramp who stands and gazes;
And there is the green for stringing the daisies!
Here is a cart run away in the road
Lumping along with man and load;
And here is a mill, and there is a river:
Each a glimpse and gone for ever!

WINTER-TIME

Late lies the wintry sun a-bed,
A frosty, fiery sleepy-head;
Blinks but an hour or two; and then,
A blood-red orange, sets again.

Before the stars have left the skies,
At morning in the dark I rise;
And shivering in my nakedness,
By the cold candle, bathe and dress.

Close by the jolly fire I sit
To warm my frozen bones a bit;
Or with a reindeer-sled, explore
The colder countries round the door.

When, to go out, my nurse doth wrap
Me in my comforter and cap:
The cold wind burns my face, and blows
Its frosty pepper up my nose.

Black are my steps on silver sod;
Thick blows my frosty breath abroad;
And tree and house, and hill and lake,
Are frosted like a wedding-cake.

Through all the pleasant meadow-side
    The grass grew shoulder-high,
Till the shining scythes went far and wide
    And cut it down to dry.

These green and sweetly smelling drops
    They led in waggons home;
And they piled them here in mountain tops
    For mountaineers to roam.

Here is Mount Clear, Mount Rusty-Nail,
    Mount Eagle and Mount High; –
The mice that in these mountains dwell,
    No happier are than I!

O what a joy to clamber there,
    O what a place for play,
With the sweet, the dim, the dusty air,
    The happy hills of hay.

FAREWELL TO THE FARM

The coach is at the door at last;
The eager children, mounting fast
And kissing hands, in chorus sing:
Good-bye, good-bye, to everything!

To house and garden, field and lawn,
The meadow-gates we swang upon,
To pump and stable, tree and swing,
Good-bye, good-bye, to everything!

And fare you well for evermore,
O ladder at the hayloft door,
O hayloft where the cobwebs cling,
Good-bye, good-bye, to everything!

Crack goes the whip, and off we go;
The trees and houses smaller grow;
Last, round the woody turn we swing:
Good-bye, good-bye, to everything!

— NORTH-WEST PASSAGE —

1. *Good Night*

When the bright lamp is carried in,
The sunless hours again begin;
O'er all without, in field and lane,
The haunted night returns again.

Now we behold the embers flee
About the firelit hearth; and see
Our faces painted as we pass,
Like pictures, on the window-glass.

Must we to bed indeed? Well then,
Let us arise and go like men,
And face with an undaunted tread
The long black passage up to bed.

Farewell, O brother, sister, sire!
O pleasant party round the fire!
The songs you sing, the tales you tell,
Till far to-morrow, fare ye well!

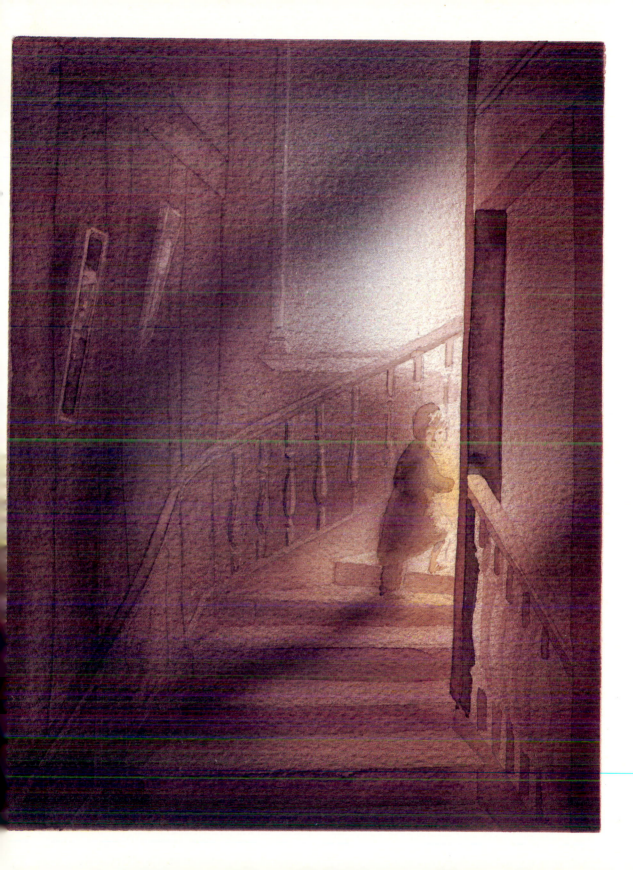

2. *Shadow March*

All round the house is the jet-black night;
    It stares through the window-pane;
It crawls in the corners, hiding from the light,
    And it moves with the moving flame.

Now my little heart goes a-beating like a drum,
    With the breath of the Bogie in my hair;
And all round the candle the crooked shadows come
    And go marching along up the stair.

The shadow of the balusters, the shadow of the lamp,
    The shadow of the child that goes to bed –
All the wicked shadows coming, tramp, tramp, tramp,
    With the black light overhead.

3. *In Port*

Last, to the chamber where I lie
My fearful footsteps patter nigh,
And come from out the cold and gloom
Into my warm and cheerful room.

There, safe arrived, we turn about
To keep the coming shadows out,
And close the happy door at last
On the perils that we past.

Then, when mamma goes by to bed,
She shall come in with tip-toe tread,
And see me lying warm and fast
And in the Land of Nod at last.

The Child Alone

THE UNSEEN PLAYMATE

When children are playing alone on the green,
In comes the playmate that never was seen.
When children are happy and lonely and good,
The Friend of the Children comes out of the wood.

Nobody heard him and nobody saw,
His is a picture you never could draw,
But he's sure to be present, abroad or at home,
When children are happy and playing alone.

He lies in the laurels, he runs on the grass,
He sings when you tinkle the musical glass;
Whene'er you are happy and cannot tell why,
The Friend of the Children is sure to be by!

He loves to be little, he hates to be big,
'Tis he that inhabits the caves that you dig;
'Tis he when you play with your soldiers of tin
That sides with the Frenchmen and never can win.

'Tis he, when at night you go off to your bed,
Bids you go to your sleep and not trouble your head;
For wherever they're lying, in cupboard or shelf,
'Tis he will take care of your playthings himself!

O it's I that am the captain of a tidy little ship,
　　Of a ship that goes a-sailing on the pond;
And my ship it keeps a-turning all around and all about;
But when I'm a little older, I shall find the secret out
　　How to send my vessel sailing on beyond.

For I mean to grow as little as the dolly at the helm,
　　And the dolly I intend to come alive;
And with him beside to help me, it's a-sailing I shall go,
It's a-sailing on the water, when the jolly breezes blow
　　And the vessel goes a divie-divie dive.

O it's then you'll see me sailing through the rushes
　　and the reeds,
　　And you'll hear the water singing at the prow;
For beside the dolly sailor, I'm to voyage and explore,
To land upon the island where no dolly was before,
　　And to fire the penny cannon in the bow.

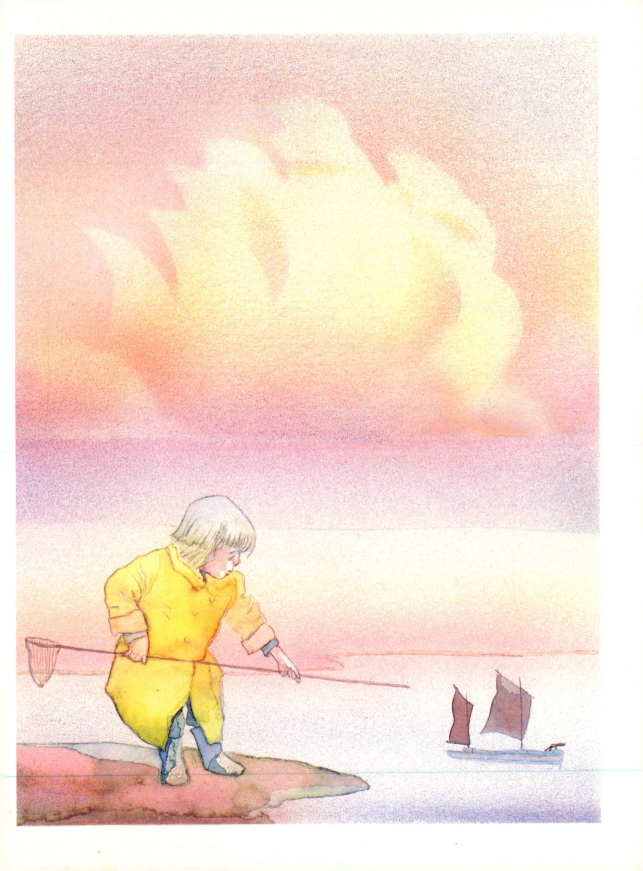

MY KINGDOM

Down by a shining water well
I found a very little dell,
    No higher than my head.
The heather and the gorse about
In summer bloom were coming out,
    Some yellow and some red.

I called the little pool a sea;
The little hills were big to me;
    For I am very small.
I made a boat, I made a town,
I searched the caverns up and down,
    And named them one and all.

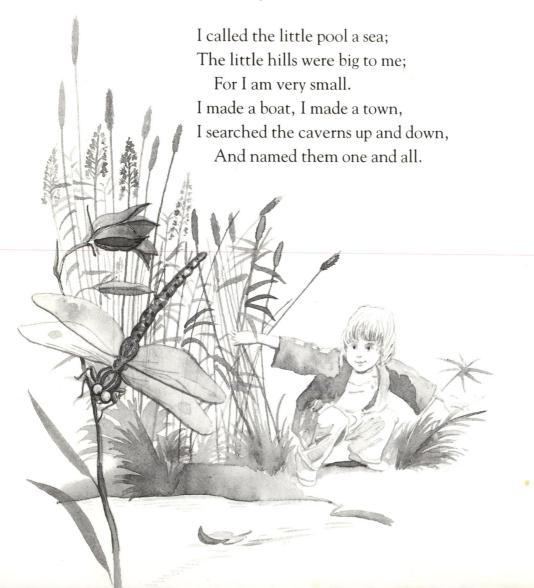

And all about was mine, I said,
The little sparrows overhead,
    The little minnows too.
This was the world and I was king;
For me the bees came by to sing,
    For me the swallows flew.

I played there were no deeper seas,
Nor any wider plains than these,
    No other kings than me.
At last I heard my mother call
Out from the house at even-fall,
    To call me home to tea.

And I must rise and leave my dell,
And leave my dimpled water well,
    And leave my heather blooms.
Alas! and as my home I neared,
How very big my nurse appeared,
    How great and cool the rooms!

PICTURE-BOOKS IN WINTER

Summer fading, winter comes –
Frosty mornings, tingling thumbs,
Window robins, winter rooks,
And the picture story-books.

Water now is turned to stone
Nurse and I can walk upon;
Still we find the flowing brooks
In the picture story-books.

All the pretty things put by,
Wait upon the children's eye,
Sheep and shepherds, trees and crooks,
In the picture story-books.

We may see how all things are,
Seas and cities, near and far,
And the flying fairies' looks,
In the picture story-books.

How am I to sing your praise,
Happy chimney-corner days,
Sitting safe in nursery nooks,
Reading picture story-books?

MY TREASURES

These nuts that I keep in the back of the nest
Where all my lead soldiers are lying at rest,
Were gathered in autumn by nursie and me
In a wood with a well by the side of the sea.

This whistle we made (and how clearly it sounds!)
By the side of a field at the end of the grounds.
Of a branch of a plane, with a knife of my own,
It was nursie who made it, and nursie alone!

The stone, with the white and yellow and grey,
We discovered I cannot tell *how* far away;
And I carried it back although weary and cold,
For though father denies it, I'm sure it is gold.

But of all my treasures the last is the king,
For there's very few children possess such a thing;
And that is a chisel, both handle and blade,
Which a man who was really a carpenter made.

BLOCK CITY

What are you able to build with your blocks?
Castle and palaces, temples and docks.
Rain may keep raining, and others go roam,
but I can be happy and building at home.

Let the sofa be mountains, the carpet be sea,
There I'll establish a city for me:
A kirk and a mill and a palace beside,
And a harbour as well where my vessels may ride

Great is the palace with pillar and wall,
A sort of tower on the top of it all,
And steps coming down in an orderly way
To where my toy vessels lie safe in the bay.

This one is sailing and that one is moored:
Hark to the song of the sailors on board!
And see on the steps of my palace, the kings
Coming and going with presents and things!

Now I have done with it, down let it go!
All in a moment the town is laid low.
Block upon block lying scattered and free,
What is there left of my town by the sea?

Yet as I saw it, I see it again,
The kirk and the palace, the ships and the men,
And as long as I live, and where'er I may be,
I'll always remember my town by the sea.

THE LAND OF STORY-BOOKS

At evening when the lamp is lit,
Around the fire my parents sit;
They sit at home and talk and sing,
And do not play at anything.

Now, with my little gun, I crawl
All in the dark along the wall,
And follow round the forest track
Away behind the sofa back.

There, in the night, where none can spy,
All in my hunter's camp I lie,
And play at books that I have read
Till it is time to go to bed.

These are the hills, these are the woods,
These are my starry solitudes;
And there the river by whose brink
The roaring lions come to drink.

I see the others far away
As if in firelit camp they lay,
And I, like to an Indian scout,
Around their party prowled about.

So, when my nurse comes in for me,
Home I return across the sea,
And go to bed with backward looks
At my dear land of Story-books.

—— ARMIES IN THE FIRE ——

The lamps now glitter down the street;
Faintly sound the falling feet;
And the blue even slowly falls
About the garden trees and walls.

Now in the falling of the gloom
The red fire paints the empty room:
And warmly on the roof it looks,
And flickers on the backs of books.

Armies march by tower and spire
Of cities blazing, in the fire;
Till as I gaze with staring eyes,
The armies fade, the lustre dies.

Then once again the glow returns;
Again the phantom city burns;
And down the red-hot valley, lo!
The phantom armies marching go!

Blinking embers, tell me true,
Where are those armies marching to,
And what the burning city is
That crumbles in your furnaces!

— THE LITTLE LAND —

When at home alone I sit
And am very tired of it,
I have just to shut my eyes
To go sailing through the skies –
To go sailing far away
To the pleasant Land of Play;
To the fairy land afar
Where the Little People are;
Where the clover-tops are trees,
And the rain-pools are the seas,
And the leaves like little ships
Sail about on tiny trips;
And above the daisy tree
   Through the grasses,
High o'erhead the Bumble Bee
   Hums and passes.

In that forest to and fro
I can wander, I can go;
See the spider and the fly,
And the ants go marching by
Carrying parcels with their feet
Down the green and grassy street.
I can in the sorrel sit,

Where the ladybird alit.
I can climb the jointed grass,
    And on high
See the greater swallows pass
    In the sky,
And the round sun rolling by
Heeding no such things as I.

Through that forest I can pass
Till, as in a looking glass,
Humming fly and daisy tree
And my tiny self I see,
Painted very clear and neat
On the rain-pool at my feet.
Should a leaflet come to land
Drifting near to where I stand,
Straight I'll board that tiny boat
Round the rain-pool sea to float.

Little thoughtful creatures sit
On the grassy coast of it.
Little things with lovely eyes
See me sailing with surprise.
Some are clad in armour green –
(These have sure to battle been!) –
Some are pied with every hue,
Black and crimson, gold and blue;
Some have wings and swift are gone;
But they all look kindly on.

When my eyes I once again
Open, and see all things plain:
High bare walls, great bare floor;
Great big knobs on drawer and door;
Great big people perched on chairs,
Stitching tucks and mending tears,
Each a hill that I could climb,
And talking nonsense all the time –
   O dear me,
   That I could be
A sailor on the rain-pool sea,
A climber in the clover tree,
And just come back, a sleepy-head,
Late at night to go to bed.

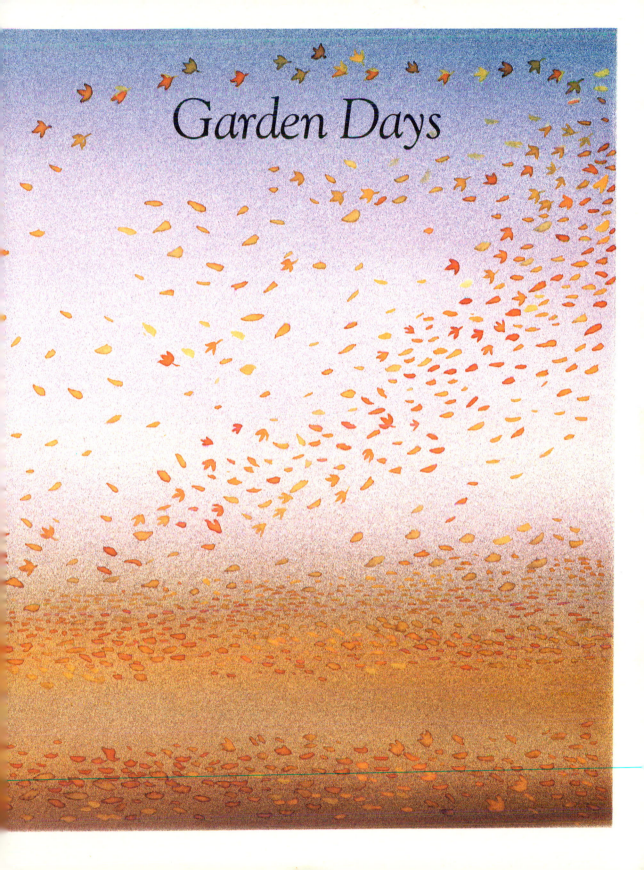

Garden Days

NIGHT AND DAY

When the golden day is done,
    Through the closing portal,
Child and garden, flower and sun,
    Vanish all things mortal.

As the blinding shadows fall,
    As the rays diminish,
Under evening's cloak, they all
    Roll away and vanish.

Garden darkened, daisy shut,
    Child in bed, they slumber –
Glow-worm in the highway rut,
    Mice among the lumber.

In the darkness houses shine,
    Parents move with candles;
Till, on all, the night divine
    Turns the bedroom handles.

Till at last the day begins
    In the east a-breaking,
In the hedges and the whins
    Sleeping birds a-waking.

In the darkness shapes of things,
    Houses, trees, and hedges,
Clearer grow; and sparrow's wings
    Beat on window ledges.

These shall wake the yawning maid;
    She the door shall open –
Finding dew on garden glade
    And the morning broken.

There my garden grows again
    Green and rosy painted,
As at eve behind the pane
    From my eyes it fainted.

Just as it was shut away,
    Toy-like, in the even,
Here I see it glow with day
    Under glowing heaven.

Every path and every plot,
    Every bush of roses,
Every blue forget-me-not
    Where the dew reposes,

'Up!' they cry, 'the day is come
    On the smiling valleys;
We have beat the morning drum;
    Playmate, join your allies!'

— NEST EGGS —

Birds all the sunny day
    Flutter and quarrel
Here in the arbour-like
    Tent of the laurel.

Here in the fork
    The brown nest is seated;
Four little blue eggs
    The mother keeps heated.

While we stand watching her,
    Staring like gabies,
Safe in each egg are the
    Bird's little babies.

Soon the frail eggs they shall
    Chip, and upspringing
Make all the April woods
    Merry with singing.

Younger than we are,
    O children, and frailer,
Soon in blue air they'll be
    Singer and sailor.

We, so much older,
    Taller and stronger,
We shall look down on the
    Birdies no longer.

They shall go flying
    With musical speeches
High overhead in the
    Tops of the beeches.

In spite of our wisdom
    And sensible talking,
We on our feet must go
    Plodding and walking.

THE FLOWERS

All the names I know from nurse:
Gardener's garters, Shepherd's purse,
Bachelor's buttons, Lady's smock,
And the Lady Hollyhock.

Fairy places, fairy things,
Fairy woods where the wild bee wings,
Tiny trees for tiny dames –
These must all be fairy names!

Tiny woods below whose boughs
Shady fairies weave a house;
Tiny tree-tops, rose or thyme,
Where the braver fairies climb!

Fair are grown-up people's trees,
But the fairest woods are these;
Where if I were not so tall,
I should live for good and all.

SUMMER SUN

Great is the sun, and wide he goes
Through empty heaven without repose;
And in the blue and glowing days
More thick than rain he showers his rays.

Though closer still the blinds we pull
To keep the shady parlour cool,
Yet he will find a chink or two
To slip his golden fingers through.

The dusty attic, spider-clad,
He, through the keyhole, maketh glad;
And through the broken edge of tiles,
Into the laddered hayloft smiles.

Meantime his golden face around
He bares to all the garden ground,
And sheds a warm and glittering look
Among the ivy's inmost nook.

Above the hills, along the blue,
Round the bright air with footing true,
To please the child, to paint the rose,
The gardener of the World, he goes.

— THE DUMB SOLDIER —

When the grass was closely mown,
Walking on the lawn alone,
In the turf a hole I found
And hid a soldier underground.

Spring and daisies came apace;
Grasses hide my hiding-place;
Grasses run like a green sea
O'er the lawn up to my knee.

Under grass alone he lies,
Looking up with leaden eyes,
Scarlet coat and pointed gun,
To the stars and to the sun.

When the grass is ripe like grain,
When the scythe is stoned again,

When the lawn is shaven clear,
Then my hole shall reappear.

I shall find him, never fear,
I shall find my grenadier;
But for all that's gone and come,
I shall find my soldier dumb.

He has lived, a little thing,
In the grassy woods of spring;
Done, if he could tell me true,
Just as I should like to do.

He has seen the starry hours
And the springing of the flowers;
And the fairy things that pass
In the forests of the grass.

In the silence he has heard
Talking bee and ladybird,
and the butterfly has flown
O'er him as he lay alone.

Not a word will he disclose,
Not a word of all he knows.
I must lay him on the shelf,
And make up the tale myself.

— AUTUMN FIRES —

In the other gardens
   And all up the vale,
From the autumn bonfires
   See the smoke trail!

Pleasant summer over
   And all the summer flowers,
The red fire blazes,
   The grey smoke towers.

Sing a song of seasons!
   Something bright in all!
Flowers in the summer,
   Fires in the fall!

THE GARDENER

The gardener does not love to talk,
He makes me keep the gravel walk;
And when he puts his tools away,
He locks the door and takes the key.

Away behind the currant row
Where no one else but cook may go,
Far in the plots, I see him dig,
Old and serious, brown and big.

He digs the flowers, green, red, and blue,
Nor wishes to be spoken to.
He digs the flowers and cuts the hay,
And never seems to want to play.

Silly gardener! summer goes,
And winter comes with pinching toes,
When in the garden bare and brown
You must lay your barrow down.

Well now, and while the summer stays,
To profit by these garden days,
O how much wiser you would be
To play at Indian wars with me!

HISTORICAL ASSOCIATIONS

Dear Uncle Jim, this garden ground
That now you smoke you pipe around
Has seen immortal actions done
And valiant battles lost and won.

Here we had best on tip-toe tread,
While I for safety march ahead,
For this is that enchanted ground
Where all who loiter slumber sound.

Here is the sea, here is the sand,
Here is simple Shepherd's Land,
Here are the fairy hollyhocks,
And there are Ali Baba's rocks.

But yonder, see! apart and high,
Frozen Siberia lies; where I,
With Robert Bruce and William Tell,
Was bound by an enchanter's spell.

There, then, awhile in chains we lay,
In wintry dungeons, far from day;
But ris'n at length, with might and main,
Our iron fetters burst in twain,

Then all the horns were blown in town;
And, to the ramparts clanging down,
All the giants leaped to horse
And charged behind us through the gorse.

On we rode, the others and I,
Over the mountains blue, and by
The Silent River, the sounding sea,
And the robber woods of Tartary.

A thousand miles we galloped fast,
And down the witches' lane we passed,
And rode amain, with brandished sword,
Up to the middle, through the ford.

Last we drew rein – a weary three –
Upon the lawn, in time for tea,
And from our steeds alighted down
Before the gates of Babylon.

Envoys

— TO WILLIE AND HENRIETTA —

If two may read aright
These rhymes of old delight
And house and garden play,
You two, my cousins, and you only, may.

You in a garden green
With me were king and queen,
Were hunter, soldier, tar,
And all the thousand things that children are.

Now in the elders' seat
We rest with quiet feet,
And from the window-bay
We watch the children, our successors, play.

'Time was,' the golden head
Irrevocably said;
But time which none can bind,
While flowing fast away, leaves love behind.

TO MY MOTHER

You too, my mother, read my rhymes
For the love of unforgotten times,
And you may chance to hear once more
The little feet along the floor.

TO AUNTIE

Chief of our aunts – not only I,
But all your dozen of nurslings cry –
What did the other children do?
And what were childhood, wanting you?

The red room with the giant bed
Where none but elders laid their head;
The little room where you and I
Did for awhile together lie
And, simple suitor, I you hand
In decent marriage did demand;
The great day nursery, best of all,
With pictures pasted on the wall
And leaves upon the blind –
A pleasant room wherein to wake
And hear the leafy garden shake
And rustle in the wind –
And pleasant there to lie in bed
And see the pictures overhead –
The wars about Sebastopol,
The grinning guns along the wall,
The daring escalade,
The plunging ships, the bleating sheep,
The happy children ankle-deep
And laughing as they wade;
All these are vanished clean away,
And the old manse is changed to-day;
It wears an altered face
And shields a stranger race.

The river, on from mill to mill,
Flows past our childhood's garden still;
But ah! we children never more
Shall watch it from the water-door!
Below the yew – it still is there –
Our phantom voices haunt the air
As we were still at play,
And I can hear them call and say:
'How far is it to Babylon?'

Ah, far enough, my dear,
Far, far enough from here –
Yet you have farther gone!
'Can I get there by candlelight?'
So goes the old refrain.
I do not know – perchance you might –
But only, children, hear it right,
Ah, never to return again!
The eternal dawn, beyond a doubt,
Shall break on hill and plain,
And put all stars and candles out,
Ere we be young again.

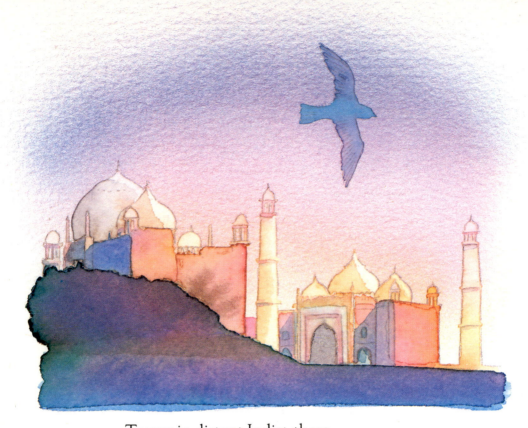

To you in distant India, these
I send across the seas,
Nor count it far across.
For which of us forgets
The Indian cabinets,
The bones of antelope, the wings of albatross.
The pied and painted birds and beans,
The junks and bangles, beads and screens,
The gods and sacred bells,
And the loud-humming, twisted shells?
The level of the parlour floor
Was honest, homely, Scottish shore;
But when we climbed upon a chair,
Behold the gorgeous East was there!

Be this a fable; and behold
Me in the parlour as of old,
And Minnie just above me set
In the quaint Indian cabinet!
Smiling and kind, you grace a shelf
Too high for me to reach myself.
Reach down a hand, my dear, and take
These rhymes for old acquaintance' sake.

I

Some day soon this rhyming volume, if you learn with
   proper speed,
Little Louis Sanchez, will be given you to read.
Then shall you discover, that your name was printed down
By the English printers, long before, in London town.

In the great and busy city where the East and West are
   met,
All the little letters did the English printer set;
While you thought of nothing, and were still too young
   to play,
Foreign people thought of you in places far away.

Ay, and while you slept, a baby, over all the English lands
Other little children took the volume in their hands;
Other children questioned, in their homes across the seas:
Who was Little Louis, won't you tell us, mother, please?

Now that you have spelt your lesson, lay it down and go
    and play,
Seeking shells and seaweed on the sands of Monterey,
Watching all the mighty whalebones, lying buried by the
    breeze,
Tiny sandy-pipers, and the huge Pacific seas.

And remember in your playing, as the sea-fog rolls to you,
Long ere you could read it, how I told you what to do;
And that while you thought of no one, nearly half the
    world away
Some one thought of Louis on the beach of Monterey!

TO ANY READER

As from the house your mother sees
You playing round the garden trees,
So you may see, if you will look
Through the windows of this book,
Another child, far, far away,
And in another garden, play.
But do not think you can at all,
By knocking on the window, call
That child to hear you. He intent
Is all on his play-business bent.
He does not hear; he will not look,
Nor yet be lured out of his book.
For, long ago, the truth to say,
He has grown up and gone away,
And it is but a child of air
That lingers in the garden there.

— INDEX OF FIRST LINES —

A birdie with a yellow bill, 55
A child should always say what's true, 20
All night long, and every night, 19
All round the house is the jet-black night, 68
All the names I know from nurse, 98
As from the house your mother sees, 118
At evening when the lamp is lit, 83

Birds all the sunny day, 96
Bring the comb and play upon it, 40

Chief of our aunts – not only I, 111
Children, you are very little, 46
Come up here, O dusty feet, 58

Dark brown is the river, 30
Dear Uncle Jim, this garden ground, 104
Down by a shining water well, 76

Every night my prayers I say, 36

Faster than fairies, faster than witches, 60
From breakfast on all though the day, 33

Great is the sun, and wide he goes, 99

How do you like to go up in a swing, 54

I have a little shadow that goes in and out with me, 34
I saw you toss the kites on high, 43
I should like to rise and go, 25
I woke before the morning, I was happy all the day, 37
If two may read aright, 109
In the other gardens, 102
In winter I get up at night, 17
It is very nice to think, 17

Last, to the chamber where I lie, 69
Late lies the wintry sun a-bed, 61
Little Indian, Sioux or Crow, 48

My bed is like a little boat, 52
My tea is nearly ready and the sun has left the sky, 50

O it's I that am the captain of a tidy little ship, 74
Of speckled eggs the birdie sings, 28
Over the borders, a sin without pardon, 44

Smooth it slides upon its travel, 56
Some day soon this rhyming volume,
   if you learn with proper speed, 116
Summer fading, winter comes, 78

The coach is at the door at last, 65
The friendly cow, all red and white, 41
The gardener does not love to talk, 103
The lamps now glitter down the street, 85
The lights from the parlour and kitchen shone out, 38
The moon has a face like the clock in the hall, 53
The rain is raining all around, 20
The red room with the giant bed, 112
The sun is not a-bed when I, 49
The world is so full of a number of things, 42
These nuts that I keep in the back of the nest, 80
Three of us afloat in the meadow by the swing, 21
Through all the pleasant meadow-side, 64

Up into the cherry-tree, 22

We built a ship upon the stairs, 29
What are you able to build with your blocks? 81
When at home alone I sit, 86
When children are playing alone on the green, 73
When I am grown to man's estate, 28
When I was down beside the sea, 18
When I was sick and lay a-bed, 31
When the bright lamp is carried in, 66

When the golden day is done, 93
When the grass was closely mown, 100
Whenever Auntie moves around, 30
Whenever the moon and stars are set, 24

You too, my mother, read my rhymes, 110